Betting Systems That Win!

GREYHOUND RACING

D1102345

Betting Systems That Win!

GREYHOUND RACING

by Statistician

foulsham

LONDON · NEW YORK · TORONTO · SYDNEY

foulsham

Bennetts Close, Cippenham, Berkshire, SL1 5AP

ISBN 0–572–01696–4

Copyright © 1991 W. Foulsham & Co Ltd.

Printed in Great Britain by
St Edmundsbury Press Ltd., Bury St Edmunds, Suffolk

CONTENTS

INTRODUCTION

Ever since the first organised greyhound racing meeting at Belle Vue, Manchester in July 1926, the sport has exercised a strong fascination over large sections of the British sporting public. Every afternoon and every evening of the week when the gaming laws permit, crowds gather at one or other of the forty plus licensed National Greyhound Racing Club stadiums all over the country. There are also about sixty independent tracks, each with its own band of dedicated followers. In fact dog racing is the second most popular spectator sport in Britain.

Racing thoroughbred greyhounds is an exciting spectacle, and of course betting on the results of races is an essential part of the fun. So this book is written with two sorts of people in mind. It is an expert approach to the subject for seasoned followers of the game who might wish to improve their betting techniques. In addition it serves as an introduction to the mysteries of greyhound form and racing generally for anyone who may like to take up the sport but who is put off by its complexities.

Everyone will find in the following pages a full analysis of the entire spectrum of betting on greyhounds. Time, form, class, forecasts, trap numbers, favourites, and the best ways to stake on your selections – all are covered in a straightforward manner that anyone can understand, whatever their previous experience of the sport. Those who attend the track regularly or follow greyhound racing in their local betting shop, as well as the home enthusiast who just likes a bet on 'the Dogs' from time to time, will find plenty to interest them in this book.

There are no easy answers to the conundrum of picking greyhound winners from keenly contested races in which a split second of high-speed action at the traps or at a bend can sometimes mean the difference between winning or losing, but this book gives sound practical advice, based on a very long acquaintance with the sport, for anyone who enjoys the thrill of greyhound racing.

SYSTEM ONE

Winners on the clock: three form factors locate the fastest dogs with the best winning chances

Time is the fundamental measure of performance in greyhound racing. Unlike horse racing there are no jockeys to vary the pace at which races are run, and of course greyhounds themselves do not have the intelligence to race tactically. A dog does not 'save' itself in a race, but with few exceptions chases the hare flat out from the start, maintaining an even speed which only slows if it begins to tire near the end of a contest. This means that the time an animal is capable of over a given distance is a very accurate guide to its probable future running against other dogs whose times for that distance are also known.

So times are the basis of the grading system which is at the heart of the sport. By bringing together in a race dogs with similar recorded times, the Racing Manager is able to produce what is in effect a handicap whose outcome can be very difficult to predict. In a typical graded event the time difference between the fastest and the slowest dog is about 0.25 seconds, using recent performances as a yardstick. The scrimmaging that nearly always occurs at some point in a race is often enough to cancel out even this minimal difference.

Therefore, although time is undoubtedly the best

guide to a dog's capabilities, the comparative time test which is the foundation of conventional methods of form-reading, is fraught with difficulties as a means of consistently selecting likely winners. Basically, when he has picked out what he thinks will prove the fastest dog in a race, the time student must then make two assumptions: first, that the quickest dog is in a physical and mental condition to reproduce its best figures, and second, that any problems it may meet in running will not be sufficient to nullify its superiority on the clock. Since neither assumption is certain to be borne out by actual events, it is apparent that the time test will never be a complete answer to the puzzle of successfully backing greyhounds. On the other hand, if a dog can be found with a big advantage over its rivals, there is a fair chance that even the occurrence of negative factors will not prevent it winning. In other words in assessing time the backer has to find ways and means of beating the grader at his own game.

To do this, some experts advocate the keeping of the most elaborate records so as to build up a private handicap or index of performance based on time. They often go to enormous lengths, rating every dog at every meeting held at the track they attend, with estimated allowances for various degrees of interference, as well as the usual ones for the state of the going and for distances behind the winner. It is doubtful, however, whether all this painstaking effort is really justified in terms of the number of winners actually indicated. Apart from periodic rests, most greyhounds race every week and sometimes twice a week. In no time at all ratings which aim at being comprehensive and definitive become immensely complicated and worse, a mass of contradictions, as dogs improve or fail to show their best running from race to race.

In fact all the essential details relating to any dog's recorded times are contained in the racecard for the meeting at which it is down to run. The racecard gives a full form summary for every contestant in every race, with precise information about winning and adjusted times, stretching back over the last four, and sometimes the last six outings. This information is quite enough to give a clear picture of any animal's potential according to the time test.

However it must be said that in many cases the use made by racegoers of the information presented for their benefit is often based on ideas which are at best suspect, and at worst downright wrong-headed, for instance beginners, and not a few regulars who should know better, look no further than the calculated time figures for the outings immediately prior to the race they are trying to analyse. Calculated times always appear on the extreme right of the form line, and give figures based on the winning times of races, adjusted for going and in the case of beaten dogs, for the number of lengths behind the winner. Going allowances are determined by track officials, whilst distances at the finish are always calculated according to the standard equation, one length equals 0.08 seconds. For example:

484 METRES FLAT

Dte	Dis	Tp	Pl	By	Wnr/ 2nd	Remarks	Win Tm	Gng	Kilos	SP	Cl	Calc Tm

SMOOTH AS SILK

Dte	Dis	Tp	Pl	By	Wnr/ 2nd	Remarks	Win Tm	Gng	Kilos	SP	Cl	Calc Tm
2Ja	484	2	3	4	On Ice	SA.Crd I&4	30.93	+10	30.4	4–1	A8	31.35

So on 2 January in a race of A8 class Smooth as Silk ran third from trap 2, beaten four lengths by the winner, On Ice. On Ice won in 30.93 seconds on going that was

11

adjudged 0.10 seconds faster than normal. Smooth as Silk therefore had a calculated time of $30.93 + 0.10 + 4 \times 0.08 = 31.35$ seconds. It weighed 30.4 kilos and started at 4–1.

Compare the calculated times for each runner's last outing, the tyro reasons, and you have the ready-made winner of the race. Now it is true that such times can be used as a general pointer in support of other factors when weighing up prospects, and in the next chapter of this book a way of doing this is illustrated, but for the serious student who wants to base his betting on an in-depth analysis of time alone, approximate indications of this kind are not really adequate. Look at the racecard remarks on Smooth as Silk's performance. In unabbreviated form they read: 'slowly away, crowded first and fourth bends'. But what time would it have achieved had it got off to a good start? How much difference to its final time did the fact that it was crowded not only at the first, but also at the last bend, make? How bad was the crowding on each occasion? It is of course impossible to say, but it is certain that 31.35 is by no means an exact measure of the dog's ability against the clock. Next time out it might break quickly from the traps, avoid all trouble and win with a calculated time of say, 30.87, a difference of six lengths. In any race under review some dogs may have had a trouble-free run on their last outing, whilst others could have been checked by scrimmaging to a greater or lesser, and unquantifiable extent. It follows that a simple comparison of last time out calculated times is at best a rough guide which the expert clock-watcher can only accept with reservations.

One possible solution is to work on average times. Adherents of this idea recommend taking an average for each dog from its last three or four runs. This, they argue, will even out the inaccuracies arising from interference in running and give a reliable figure for each competitor. Another idea along similar lines is to establish the best and worst times from a number of recent outings and strike an average of the two.

But all this really achieves is to compound the error likely to creep into a single calculated time. Instead of one possibly suspect figure, two, three or four are taken, and the student of time ends up with the worst of all possible worlds.

Where then does the harassed punter turn? He has been told that time is the basis of the grading of races and of greyhound form generally, yet it seems that calculated times, the best that men and mathematics can devise, are liable to error to such a degree that they are unreliable as a means of picking winners.

Well, there is one sort of calculated time which is less suspect than all the others. It is a dog's very best time taken from all its recent runs. This is because the incalculable effect of interference is largely eliminated from the argument, for when a dog sets up its fastest recent time it almost certainly met either with no or the very minimum of trouble. So if we take the best recent time for each contestant in a race, we have a sound standard by which to compare them. Occasionally an animal will have been baulked every time in its last few outings, but there is not much anyone can do about this type of dog, except to say that it is one which is prone to suffer interference, and may well be impeded again. For the rest, however, the concept of fastest recent time represents the truest possible measure of known ability. A dog may improve on its best figures of course, but this is very difficult to predict from previous running. Conversely it may have an off day and fail to reproduce its form, or it may get the worst of things in a rough race.

The latter is an imponderable that lies within the realms of unpredictable chance, but few dogs deteriorate rapidly in a short period. Provided the fastest time is taken from the last three outings, which normally cover about ten days to a fortnight, there is every possibility that a dog will run close to it when it gets a reasonably clear run.

There is one further complicating factor. This is the value which the time enthusiast ought to put on the evidence of trials. Trials are useful for trainers in assessing a greyhound's progress, but they are very confusing from a backer's point of view, for a two-, three- or even a four-dog trial is quite unlike an actual race. All too often you will see a dog highly graded on the strength of a fast trial fail to repeat the figures in the real thing. The solution must be to ignore trial times altogether when analysing a competitive race.

It is now possible to formulate rules for the first part of a sound time system:

i) Consider only the last three outings, including any trials, of each dog in the race under review.
ii) Cross out trial times and times for races not over the distance of this race.
iii) The BEST TIME DOG is the one with the fastest calculated time in previous runs not eliminated by ii).
iv) In the event of a tie between the fastest times of two or more dogs, ignore the race altogether.

Here is an example of the rules in operation:

484 METRES FLAT

			Calculated Time
Trap 1	484 m.	4DT	30.85X
	484 m.	3DT	31.10X
	484 m.	Race	30.98
	484 m.	Race	31.15X
Trap 2	484 m.	Race	31.06
	484 m.	3DT	31.22X
	484 m.	2DT	30.96X
	484 m.	Race	31.03X
Trap 3	523 m.	Race	33.38X
	484 m.	Race	31.34
	484 m.	Race	31.42
	484 m.	Race	30.92X
Trap 4	484 m.	Race	31.27
	484 m.	Race	31.25
	300 m.	4DT	17.16X
	484 m.	Race	31.14X
Trap 5	484 m.	Race	31.02
	484 m.	Race	30.89
	484 m.	Race	31.21
	523 m.	3DT	33.44X
Trap 6	523 m.	Race	33.49X
	484 m.	Race	31.23
	484 m.	Solo	31.41X
	484 m.	Race	31.02X

An 'X' denotes times invalid under system rules, including all those recorded before the three outings immediately prior to the present contest. The dog in trap 1 did 30.85 last time out which is the quickest time by any competitor, but this is ignored because it was set up in a trial. The 5 dog with 30.89 on its penultimate run has the fastest time from all the races that qualify for comparison, and is the BEST TIME DOG in the race.

So far so good, but it was noted at the beginning of this chapter that it is not enough just to identify the probable fastest dog. The grader too will have taken account of a particularly good time when framing the event, and it is a fact that many dogs which record a fast time with a clear run in one grade often struggle against better class dogs in a higher grade. The quicker pace finds them out on the run to the first bend, and lacking the edge to go clear, they prove incapable of reproducing the figures they achieved in the lower grade. To get the better of the grader, and also to discount as far as possible the chance of some baulking in the course of the race, other form considerations need to be introduced. Backing the BEST TIME DOG in each graded race down the card may yield a lot of winners, but something more is required in order to single out only the outstanding bets on time. The BEST TIME DOG must also have one of several additional plus factors in its favour which may well make its time advantage decisive.

The first additional factor is as follows:

Any BEST TIME DOG now running in one grade lower than that of its last race is a system qualifier.

At most tracks the grades, or classes of race, run from A8 (the lowest) up to A1 (the highest) over the standard distance, with narrower numerical ranges for dashes, middle-distance and stayers' races, prefixed 'D', 'M' and 'S', at the bigger stadiums which have enough dogs in the kennels to feature regular competition among animals with a specialist racing distance. So if a dog which has been running in A4 races is dropped to an A5 event, it has shown that it is unable to cope with the speed of slightly classier dogs on current form. If it is nonetheless the BEST TIME DOG in recent races, this type of down-graded greyhound has an excellent chance of beating animals which have slower calculated times and which the grader recognises as inferior to the opponents it has been competing against. It quite often makes the most of the opportunity and is well worth support.

The second factor which indicates a sound investment is:

> The BEST TIME DOG is a system qualifier if it finished second in its last race, provided it has not been raised in grade as a result of that run.

In fact very few Racing Managers raise a dog in class on the strength of a second place, whatever the time of the race. If a dog leads its field on the clock over the three previous outings and beat all bar the winner last time out, it is obviously capable of winning in its current grade and may well follow up immediately with a win. Indeed this sort of dog represents one of the very best bets in graded racing, although starting prices are unlikely to be over-generous.

The third additional factor may be summarised thus:

> The BEST TIME DOG qualifies under the system if the racecard notes that it suffered interference in its most recent race and a price of 7–2 or better in

five-dog races or 4–1 or better in six-dog races is obtainable from a bookmaker or the Totalisator.

If the dog with the fastest recent time in the field was beaten last time out, there could have been a good reason for the below par display. Racecard comments like 'impeded', 'baulked', 'crowded', 'bumped' are the telltale signs. When these remarks are prefixed with the epithet 'badly', the backer has extra grounds for confidence in hoping that with a clear run, the animal may be able to repeat its best time figure and return to form, possibly winning form.

There is no guarantee of course, and that is why such dogs are only backed if a 'value' price is available from the layers or from the Tote, as indicated on its betting screens just before the dogs are loaded into the traps. By confining himself to betting at good odds, the backer has a realistic chance over a reasonable period of offsetting losses from those dogs which fail to come up to expectations, and to emerge with an overall gain.

This chapter pinpoints some of the best bets on time in greyhound racing. If you pick out only the fastest dogs with special additional factors in their favour, you may back many winners. Yet nothing is certain in a sport where not much more than a couple of seconds separates a Derby winner from the lowest grade of racer over the Classic distance. A bad bump at a key moment in a race can beat any dog with a big advantage on time and grade, and greyhounds do not always produce their best form even with an unimpeded run. Nevertheless the time test outlined above is an expert approach to finding winners in an area of the sport where many enthusiasts frequently get it wrong.

SYSTEM TWO

The fundamentals of form

There are a number of form indicators in greyhound racing which are as old as the organised sport itself. Reading form accurately is a complex art involving the analysis of a whole range of such indicators, but some have much less value than others. The object of this chapter is to steer the punter away from those of the traditional ideas which will be of little help to him in his search for winners, and to highlight several positive factors that can be applied systematically which he ignores at his peril.

Weight

From a purely betting point of view the weight of dogs is a controversial subject. At the track the runners' weights in kilos are read out over the public address system before each race, and can then, if the punter so chooses, be compared with weights for previous races as recorded on the racecard. Now it is a fact that some backers take a lively interest in weight and only bet if they are convinced their fancy fulfils certain weight requirements. They are entitled to their view of course, but even a cursory glance at any racecard will reveal that most dogs show only fractional differences in weight from race to race. It could be that an animal has an ideal racing weight which is indicative of maximum fitness, although how this is determined by the backer is a mystery to the present writer, and it is hard to believe that marginal variations make any real difference to a dog's racing performance. It is true that the Racing Management could well take a dim view of a dog that suddenly exhibits a huge fluctuation in weight in the course of a few days, for this might suggest that its trainer has been trying to reduce his charge's well-being by a severely restricted diet or by deliberate over-feeding, but in the main cheating at greyhound racing, if it occurs at all, does not take the form of such obvious and blatant manoeuvres.

Nor does the old maxim 'a good big one will always beat a good little one' have much validity as a way of predicting results. If you go racing regularly, you will see a tiny bitch out-speed a giant dog in many a race. Small greyhounds may suffer more than big ones in a very rough contest, but most of the time the avoidance of interference is far more about pace and track craft than physical size.

The study of weights, therefore, is not really a factor likely to yield much useful information when assessing prospects for a race. If the form-reader never considers weight at all, it is probable that his percentage of winning bets will not suffer one jot because of it.

Anticipating trouble

Many backers study the known characteristics of dogs in an attempt to work out which runners in a race are likely to run into trouble and which are likely to get a clear run. They can do this in one of two ways. Either they can 'read' races with a view to establishing the running styles of different animals as a reference point for the future, or they can analyse the sectional placings for past races which are featured on racecards at most of the bigger stadiums. These give the position of each dog as it left the traps, and at the first, second and third quarters of the race distance. For example:

BALLYSIMBA BOY
Trap 2   1123   4th   3l. . . . . .

Here Ballysimba Boy, starting from trap 2, came out of its box ahead of the rest of the field and was still in front at the quarter distance. By halfway, however, he had lost his lead and was running second before dropping back still further to be only third with three-quarters of the race over. At the finish he was fourth, three lengths behind the winner.

Using such information to try to estimate in advance how a race will be run is what the expert judge of form is traditionally supposed to do, and it is true that many press writers fill their copy on featured races with predictions of this sort. But in practice such analysis is more often than not proved wrong by actual events.

The reason is that with very few exceptions greyhounds are not consistent enough to allow accurate forecasts along these lines. There are certainly dogs which usually trap fast, and others that tend to leave the box slowly. There are dogs which hug the rails, some which keep a more or less straight course on the dash to the first bend, and quite a number which always run wide, preferring the outside to the 'traffic jam' at the first corner. There are 'faders' which have good early pace but come back to the field as the end of a race nears, while some dogs start slowly but often pick up ground rapidly off the final bend as the other runners tire. However, whatever the running style of an individual dog, it is not a machine and will not always exactly duplicate previously exhibited characteristics. Again, a lot depends on the strength of the opposition and the class of the event. A good starter in one grade may lag behind immediately against faster animals in a better one. A slow starter, dropped in class, may be able to lie up and even lead early on.

For these reasons few dogs have consistent sets of sectional figures from one race to another. For example:

JUDY'S DAUGHTER

Trap 3	6444	3rd	5¼l. . . . . .
Trap 2	3222	4th	3¾l. . . . . .
Trap 2	1122	2nd	1l. . . . . .
Trap 2	5421	1st	1¾l. . . . . .

What is the form student to make of this? Judy's Daughter in her last four races left the traps in a different position each time. Last time out she made little progress from a bad start. Before that, she got into a challenging position but then faded to finish fourth, but on her two previous runs stayed on strongly, once from a fast break and once from a poor one. Racecards are full of anomalies of this kind.

Given such inconsistencies in running, forecasts of how a race will be run, including the probable trouble spots, are for the most part unlikely to prove very accurate. There is one exception. If a dog which habitually runs wide is placed in an inside box, it will veer across the course and cause havoc as it meets the dogs making for the corner from the traps on its outside. This danger is so real that the sport's administrators give full recognition to the fact and seed some dogs as 'wide runners', denoted by a 'W' on the racecard. Animals of this sort must always start from a high-numbered trap, leaving the proven railers to occupy the inner boxes. Apart from this, in many actual races if only one dog fails to behave in the expected way, there is every chance of a completely different scenario to the one to be forecast from a study of each contestant's running characteristics. The theory behind the idea is fine, but in reality a melee of tightly bunched dogs racing round bends is not a predictable quantity, and the punter will do well to leave this kind of calculation out of his betting plans.

Speed to the first bend

At any track there are numerous examples every year of dogs fading in a race after leading early, but it is also a fact that many, many races are won by animals which lead at the first bend. They avoid any scrimmaging behind them, and even fast-finishing dogs are always struggling to get on terms in the middle of a race. Often the initial advantage proves decisive. Conversely, a dog which starts slowly from an inside box seldom wins because it emerges from the first corner behind a wall of dogs and is never able to get into a challenging position.

There are quite a few backers, therefore, who will not bet on a dog unless they are convinced it will be in front at the first bend. This idea is also the origin of several systems. Some punters look for a fast starter drawn between two slow ones in the belief that this indicates an animal likely to gain a vital early advantage. Others make a practice of trying to pick out the dog they think will break fastest from the three inside traps and back it for a win and a place. Another popular method is to make a list of proven fast starters and follow them on a staking plan from race to race.

This is all very well in theory, but the same kind of objections apply here as to attempts to estimate which runners have the best chance of avoiding interference by studying running styles. Even fast trappers 'sleep' in the boxes from time to time and do not always come out in front. When they do get away quickly, this is no guarantee of a decisive first bend lead should another animal get a 'flier' from its box. Upgraded, they may well prove incapable of capitalising on their initial speed against pacier dogs which are consistently faster over the whole distance of the race, including possibly the first few metres.

Speed to the bend is certainly an important factor in any contest, but except in the case of a really brilliant greyhound, most dogs cannot be absolutely relied on to lead early. Dogs of average ability are just not that consistent, and in any case they still have to maintain any early advantage right up to the finishing line. Their ability to do so depends ultimately on their current form in relation to the strength of the opposition, not merely on their pace at the start of a race.

Bitches

Bitches when they are at their peak are much more reliable than dogs. They show more determination in their races, running on truly to the end, a phenomenon underlined by the fact that as a general rule they make the best stayers over long distances.

However bitches display great variations in form. This is because of their seasonal cycle. They come into season twice a year. They have a tendency to run well just before they do so, and then, mated or not, are prohibited by the rules from competing for ten weeks. When they do come back to racing they nearly always perform indifferently, but sometime after the seventeenth week from their seasonal date they begin to show sudden and dramatic improvement, and will often beat the grader time and again. This is the best time to support them with hard cash. The tactic is not difficult. Keep an eye on the date a good bitch came into season. This

24

information is recorded on the racecard. Four months later note her times for signs of a revival. A rapid improvement against the clock heralds a return to form, frequently in spectacular fashion, and the astute backer can cash in, often at good prices, for many followers of the sport do not take such a long view and judge bitches only on their poor runs in the weeks following their return to competition.

Age

To anybody who does not study greyhound racing closely, the age of a dog may not seem very important. However racing dogs are just like any other type of athlete. They gradually build up to a physical peak at about the same age, maintain it for a period of time when they are at the height of their powers, then begin to deteriorate. The age cycle has in fact a considerable bearing on greyhound racing, not only as a general trend, but in terms of assessing individual races.

Dogs are officially puppies until they reach their second birthday. From the age of fifteen months when they are introduced to racing, all young dogs come on by leaps and bounds physically. The best of them improve rapidly as racers, but all puppies, even the precocious ones, are risky betting propositions. They have not yet learnt to trap consistently and often lose ground at the start. Against older dogs they frequently lack the strength and sturdiness to hold their own in a rough race and are always vulnerable at the bends. Physical attributes apart, sheer inexperience will beat a puppy on many occasions when strictly on merit it is improving enough to beat its seniors. The remedy is obvious. The wise punter will do well to steer clear of any young dog until it has attained the age of two, even if it appears to hold a decisive form advantage, when the best policy will be to leave the race alone as a betting medium.

On the other hand an animal over four years of age is definitely past its best for racing purposes, and in a large number of cases the deterioration begins approximately six months before. Every animal is an individual, but old dogs are best ignored when weighing up prospects in a race. They will have acquired a great deal of racing know-how in the course of their careers, but the vital edge has gone off their speed. The most that can be said in their favour is that they are often good value for place bets because they return very consistent times, but they seldom manage to win against younger, more enthusiastic animals at the top of their racing ability.

The month and year of whelping for every dog is shown on racecards, and this is a piece of information that has an important bearing on results. It is not suggested that the backer should try to pick winners on age alone, but he will avoid a great many poor wagers if he adheres strictly to the golden rule of never backing an animal which is under two and more than three and a half years old.

Time

In the opening chapter of this book there was a detailed explanation of a complete time test designed to find winners exclusively on the clock, but the form-reader can use times in a more straightforward manner as a controlling factor in support of other indicators as a way of eliminating many losing bets.

A veteran of greyhound racing whose experience stretches back to the very earliest days of the sport once told me that although he agreed that best recent times were the most accurate guide to greyhound form, nevertheless in many races it is possible to leave out half the field simply by examining times recorded last time out. Fascinated, I set about checking the idea and was amazed to discover the truth of his assertion.

Below I show the results of a survey of five hundred graded, six-dog races at an important London venue. The dogs were assessed by their calculated time on their previous run, after adjustment for distance behind the winner and for the official going allowance, that is the figure which appears on the far right of the racecard form line. Since the concept implied a study of only the most recent time available, trial figures were included.

500 Graded Races
Two fastest dogs won 41% (33%)
Three fastest dogs won 71% (50%)
Four fastest dogs won 81% (66%)

In brackets is shown the strictly mathematical winning expectation for each group in a six-dog race. A comparison between actual races won and the mathematical expectation makes it clear that it is the middle figure which is most instructive in terms of measuring winning potential by the simple method of using recorded times last time out. The three fastest dogs won 21% more races than they should really have done treating the runners as three numbers out of six, compared with only 8% over the odds for the two fastest animals and 15% for the four fastest. Clearly the two slowest dogs on the most recent clocking have a poor statistical chance.

It is not suggested that a dog with a very slow time which encountered severe interference in its last race should always be eliminated by this idea, but the above figures are very impressive, and as a rough check this little time test can be very useful in locating the runners with the best prospects. The method will certainly cut out some winners from your form selections, but it should get rid of a far greater number of potential losers.

Reading form is not an exact science, and there are no absolute 'rights' and 'wrongs' in the analysis of chancy contests between racing dogs. This chapter is at times heretical in the sense that it tries to refute part of traditional greyhound betting lore, and readers will have their own ideas about how to find winners 'on the book', but anyone who incorporates the above assessments into his betting will at least be adopting a logical and consistent approach which may point him in the right direction much more often than not.

SYSTEM THREE

A ratings method which automatically pinpoints likely winners and probable losers

Conventional analysis of greyhound form is concerned with relating time to grade, and is discussed in other sections of this book. However, different approaches to reading form are possible. Form figures, the placings of an animal in its last three or last six outings, are commonplace as a guide to future performance in horse racing. Indeed certain form figures, if followed consistently over a period of time, can show small level stakes profits. In greyhound sport, purists would argue, this relatively straightforward approach is useless. The constant re-grading of dogs on the basis of time in relation to the class of the opposition renders form figures suspect, the more so as the final placings in a lot of races are affected by scrimmaging at the bends.

However, if we look closely at sets of performance figures for greyhound races at different levels of competition, an interesting picture emerges.

First, here are examples from the four lowest graded races at four recent meetings at a London venue which happen to be before me as I write. Each pair of figures shows the finishing positions of the sixteen winning dogs in the two outings immediately before their successful run, with the most recent performance on the right:

55	25	23	54
64	46	16	61
52	34	25	34
23	63	64	43

These figures are absolutely typical and show a preponderance of fourths, fifths and sixths over better placings, with relatively few firsts and seconds. They demonstrate quite clearly that at the lower end of the greyhound spectrum, poor form figures are no barrier to a winning run.

However, if we look at a similar block of results for the four highest graded races at the same four meetings, things improve dramatically:

52	23	12	25
21	26	31	22
11	41	22	43
46	52	51	32

Here there are only two sixths in the entire set of figures, with five winners last time out, and firsts, seconds and thirds occurring twenty-three times out of a possible thirty-two. In fact only one pair (46) contains no placing in the first three at all.

Turning to open races, where the grading system does not operate, the case for good form figures as a prerequisite of success is even more impressive. Below are the previous placings of the winners of sixteen open races taken at random. I emphasise that they have been extracted from the sporting press over a few nights of racing with no attempt to 'pick and choose' merely to prove a point.

11	35	16	16
11	11	21	21
22	11	12	31
12	16	22	21

From these returns it is evident that good form figures are an essential part of the credentials of winners in the very top echelon of the sport.

Clearly the higher the level of the race, the better the form figures exhibited by winners in their previous runs. To that extent, performance figures do have some relevance to greyhound racing. But, non-graded open races apart, the trouble with the concept of previous placings as a possible indicator of future running is that in isolation they do not take into account the class of event in which a particular figure was achieved. What is needed is some system that relates finishing position to the grade of race.

Fortunately there is a fairly simple way of doing this, although most greyhound enthusiasts are probably not familiar with it. The grading formula used in this country is sometimes called the 'Wimbledon' system, because it was at that track where it was originally perfected and developed many years ago. The system in its complete form allows for ten grades over the standard track distance, A1 to A10, and whilst time was used as the basic bench mark, a method of assessing overall class in relation to performance was also evolved which could be employed as a check on gradings based on recorded clockings.

The basis of the method is the following table:

		WON	2ND	3RD	4TH	5TH	6TH
GRADE	A1	15	14	13	12	11	10
	A2	14	13	12	11	10	9
	A3	13	12	11	10	9	8
	A4	12	11	10	9	8	7
	A5	11	10	9	8	7	6
	A6	10	9	8	7	6	5
	A7	9	8	7	6	5	4
	A8	8	7	6	5	4	3
	A9	7	6	5	4	3	2
	A10	6	5	4	3	2	1

If this table is applied to an animal's form over its last three, or possibly last four outings, it is a simple matter to arrive at a figure which accurately sums up the value of its recent form. Find the figure for each runner in a race and you have a set of automatic ratings by which prospects can be assessed according to the principle of linking previous placings to grade. The allocation of points can also be used for 'D', 'M' and 'S' events.

Here is an example of the working of the method on a race which actually took place, although for copyright reasons the names of the dogs have been changed. Only the last three races are assessed, since very recent form is the most reliable in greyhound racing:

RACE GRADED A6

Trap 1   CANDYHILL'S DARKIE
          6th in A6 =   5
          2nd in A5 = 10
          4th in A5 =   8
                      ———
                       23
                      ———

Trap 2   **CENTRE COURT**
1st in A7 =   9
3rd in A6 =   8
5th in A6 =   6
             23

Trap 3   **OLD BOND**
6th in A6 =   5
3rd in A6 =   8
1st in A7 =   9
             22

Trap 4   **SILVER GHOST**
5th in A5 =   7
5th in A5 =   7
3rd in A5 =   9
             23

Trap 5   **JET PLANE**
2nd in A6 =   9
3rd in A6 =   8
3rd in A5 =   9
             26

Trap 6   **SWIFT REASON**
3rd in A6 =   8
1st in A7 =   9
3rd in A7 =   7
             24

This was a fairly even contest according to the ratings with every runner having some sort of chance, but Jet Plane had a 2-point advantage over the rest of the field, and Swift Reason was clear next best. The result of the race was a win for Jet Plane at 4–1. Swift Reason finished second at 5–1, and the Tote forecast paid a handsome 28–1.

Obviously the method will not work out so well every time, and because of the nature of the grading system where animals are only moved up and down very gradually in class, there will rarely be big differences between the figures for the top-rated dog and the other runners in a race. However any backer employing the method can usually draw a number of important conclusions about any race he is trying to analyse. They may be summarised as follows:

  i) Any top-rated dog with a figure of 3 or more points higher than its closest rival would be an outstanding bet.
 ii) A top-rated dog with a figure 2 points higher than the second best in the race would constitute a sound bet.
iii) An advantage of 1 point over the field would indicate a dog with a fair chance of winning, although other dogs rated only slightly inferior would have real prospects of beating it.
 iv) Often several of the runners have very poor figures when compared with the best-rated dogs, and can be eliminated with some degree of confidence as 'no-hopers', although of course nothing is certain in the form of greyhounds.

v) When not more than 1 or 2 points separate the entire field, this would clearly be a closely graded race and it could well be passed over as a betting proposition.

vi) The method can be used for forecast betting, especially when two dogs appear to be much better than the rest. Here the reversed forecast Tote bet would be a powerful weapon in the punter's armoury.

The method is simple to operate, and very few problems arise in applying it, for final placings and the grade of races are always shown on racecards. Trials present a difficulty, since they are never graded, the only indication of the merit of a trial performance being the time that was recorded. The recommended procedure is to ignore trials altogether and take only the three most recent actual races of each runner.

Sometimes dogs move from one race distance to another. Although form over varying distances can be misleading, here the backer is advised to ignore the distance prefix and rate the performance according to the class number of the event. The figures for the dogs in traps 5 and 6 are an example of this procedure in the following race:

RACE GRADED M5

Trap 1   SHADOW BOXER
          2nd in M5 = 10
          4th in M4 = 9
          1st in M5 = 11
                     ——
                      30
                     ——

Trap 2   SANCHO CHAMP
5th in M5 = 7
2nd in M5 = 10
3rd in M4 = 10
            27

Trap 3   EASY TIME
6th in M5 = 6
5th in M4 = 8
1st in M5 = 11
            25

Trap 4   COME ON SANDY
4th in M4 = 9
2nd in M4 = 11
6th in M4 = 7
            27

Trap 5   HI JOHNNY
3rd in M5 = 9
2nd in A7 = 8
4th in A6 = 7
            24

Trap 6   BLACK BULLET
3rd in M5 = 9
6th in A7 = 4
2nd in A7 = 8
            21

This race was also a real one. Shadow Boxer was rated 3 points better than any other dog in the field and looked a very good bet. He won, although at a short price, but not odds on, with Hi Johnny second, so the method did not locate the winning forecast, but it did reveal quite clearly that the dog in trap 6 had very little chance.

For anyone looking for a sound, easy-to-operate way of evaluating greyhound form, with the possibility of winners and forecasts at all kinds of prices, the above ratings method has a great deal in its favour. It has nothing to do with time or any other of the usual ways of assessing form, and may often throw up good bets not apparent to other punters. Infallibility is not claimed, but by relating performance to class in a logical way, if used sensibly and selectively, it offers the thoughtful backer the opportunity to assess prospects in any race with a high level of expertise that may well produce consistent profits.

SYSTEM FOUR

The very best dogs to follow

There are many ways of backing greyhounds, but by and large most punters, whether they attend the track or place their bets in a betting shop, treat each card as a separate entity. They may bet in every race, or back a few carefully chosen dogs which they think have an outstanding chance. They employ such criteria as form, time or trap number combinations to arrive at their selections. Some bet with the bookmakers, others on the Tote. They may prefer win only betting, or use place bets to try to make small but unspectacular gains, and sometimes as a kind of insurance policy against complete loss on win stakes. The more speculatively inclined go for forecasts which offer the chance of a big return for a limited outlay. All these different approaches have something to be said for them, but none are likely to succeed in the long run unless they form part of a general betting plan.

So most greyhound punters have some good meetings and some bad. If they win, they pocket their winnings. If they lose, they mentally shrug their shoulders and hope for better things next time. There is no thought of re-investing gains or of planning for recovery of losses. If they kept an accurate record of profit and loss, and very few do, they would probably discover that they show a sizeable debit balance over an extended period of betting.

On the other hand a minority of punters do make their greyhound racing pay. They see their betting as a long term operation. One bet, or one meeting, is treated as part of a series of bets or series of meetings with an overall gain, not a quick profit, as the ultimate aim. This is the great advantage of the method described in the present chapter. It singles out certain dogs which are at the very peak of their form and recommends the backer to follow them in a planned way in their subsequent runs at future meetings. Given average luck, an overall winning balance is much more likely from this policy than from an unconnected series of hit-and-miss stabs at isolated meetings.

The idea, then, is to list good dogs and follow them. The success of the scheme will obviously depend on the winning potential of the animals chosen. Now the form of all racing dogs moves up and down in cycles, and the ones which are at or near the top of the form cycle are not easy to spot by the study of recorded times, the traditional barometer of a dog's current form. Even a rapidly improving animal will not show a steady upward curve in the times that it produces. Rather there are peaks and troughs, accounted for by good and bad luck in running, favourable and unfavourable trap placings, and above all by the class of dogs the grader puts up against it. When times alone do indicate a purple patch, everyone else will have spotted the trend with poor starting prices the inevitable result.

There is in fact a much simpler and more effective way of pinpointing dogs that are worth following in subsequent races. The key is to take careful note of the distances by which winning dogs beat their closest rivals in a race. Any animal that is well clear of its field must be worth a very close look when trying to assess prospects for the future, and the system plan is to list winners which record a winning distance of three or more lengths in graded events.

The simplicity of this idea should not disguise its merits. There are a number of possibilities in terms of what can happen to dogs with such a form qualification in subsequent runs, and if these are examined closely, it becomes apparent that the scheme has a really good chance of paying off.

A winner by a wide margin might just be allowed to remain in the same grade next time out. A lot depends on the grading policy at the particular track, but in the main only the best dogs in the kennels already in the top grade will enjoy this advantage. Clearly they have a first-rate chance of repeating their success. There is little the Racing Manager can do to halt their progress, and, as the fastest dogs at the stadium in peak form, they must be supported to win again.

On most occasions, however, a winning dog will be asked to race next time against better dogs in one grade higher. Obviously if it is a system qualifier, it will have excellent prospects in the better grade. Except for the best at the track, the vast majority of the dogs on the racing strength have a very similar overall ability. So the grade of the typical dog is based only on recent form as reflected in its recorded times. This is all a matter of few hundredths of a second, and the good winner, even when raised in class, is not facing a really difficult task. It only has to repeat its good run against hitherto slightly superior dogs on past form to come through and win again.

At a few tracks the better winners are sometimes required to face a double jump in grade. Wembley is one stadium where at the time of writing this happens regularly. Here the backer should beware. A jump of two grades is asking a lot of any dog, even one in peak form. Unless it is making vast improvement, the extra speed needed to match strides with animals currently returning much better times than those in its previous grade may well be lacking. So the basic system rule needs to be modified in this respect. Dogs which win by the three lengths plus margin are followed only if racing in the same grade one grade higher on their next run. 'Double jumpers', as they are sometimes called, are excluded.

There is another type of dog to guard against when operating the method. Some tracks feature a few handicaps with staggered starts to add variety to programmes consisting mainly of level-break racing. A small number have nothing but handicaps. What sometimes happens in a handicap is that a dog receiving distance from all the dogs in the stagger gets a flying start, and clear of any trouble behind it, streaks away to win by a wide margin. Winning dogs of this type should be avoided for system purposes. Other dogs which win really well in a handicap are worth listing, but not those which shoot off from the front box and are never headed. It is most unlikely they will be given the same opportunity again and are best forgotten.

Leaving these two exceptions aside, listed dogs are sound bets to win again in the near future. However, obviously they will not all win their next race. According to statistics from all kinds of tracks, something like 25% manage to do so. If they lose, are they worth backing again and for how long? Again intensive research suggests that many system dogs win within three subsequent outings, even if they fail on the first of these. They may need time to adjust to the higher grade before getting their heads in front, or they may be dropped back to their original grade after one or two failures against classier dogs and then recover winning form. My figures show a win within three outings for about 65% of all system qualifiers. So the rule is to give every listed dog three chances to win. After a victory or three losing races, they are deleted from the list.

Staking is clearly important. The recommendation is to put the largest stake on the next run after listing, and two smaller stakes on the next two outings in the hope of at least recovering the big stake. If prices are good, and they often are, an animal may still show an overall profit even when it needs two or three races to recover winning form. So the staking progression is 3 points to win next time out; if lose, 1 point on each subsequent outing whilst a dog is running for the system, that is for two more races, stop at a win.

How this works out in practice can be seen from the set of results below. It shows the record of a hundred system qualifiers at a six-dog track in the south of England. The figures were compiled by fixing a starting date for system operations, then listing every qualifier until a quota of one hundred was reached. In all, the results represent about four months of racing at this one track.

WON NEXT TIME OUT (Stake: 3 points. 27 winners)

2–1, 3–1, 6–4, 11–4, 4–1,
11–4, 4–1, 5–4, 6–1, 9–2,
4–1, 7–4, 7–4, 11–4, 7–2,
6–1, 7–1, 3–1, 4–1, 9–1,
6–4, 11–10, 7–4, 3–1, 5–2,
3–1, 4–1.

Profit: 274 points

WON WITHIN TWO RUNS (Stakes: 3 points, 1
                              point. 17 winners)

7–2, 4–1, 5–1, 11–4, 7–4,
5–1, 5–2, 3–1, 9–2, 7–2,
9–2, 6–1, 7–2, 7–4, 4–1,
8–1, 5–4.

Profit: 13½ points

WON WITHIN THREE RUNS (Stakes: 3 points, 1
                                point, 1 point. 21
                                winners)

5–1, 8–1, Evens, 2–1, 7–1,
3–1, 10–11, 6–4, 5–1, 5–2,
11–8, 4–1, 8–1, 9–2, 7–2,
5–2, 4–1, 3–1, 3–1, 13–2,
7–2.

Loss: 4 ⅕ points

NO WIN IN THREE RUNS (Stakes: 3 points, 1
                              points, 1 point. 35
                              losers)

Loss: 175 points

Profit overall: 108 ⅓ points
Total outlay: 429 points
Percentage profit on outlay: 25%

Betting with a bookmaker away from the track, the
punter would also have had to pay tax either on stakes
or on returns. Even for track bettors a margin of 25%
on outlay is far from spectacular. However, the returns
do show the consistency of a system which definitely

produces good winners. This is only a sample of results at one venue from a relatively short period of betting. At your own track you may do better, or since greyhounds are not mathematical machines, you could do worse.

Hence the method is not the road to instant riches. On the other hand it does yield a steady supply of winners, frequently at better-than-average prices. Easy to operate, it provides interesting and varied betting with a fair chance of a reasonable profit, but even for those who prefer not to religiously follow every qualifier, the basic idea of carefully monitoring the progress of wide-margin winners in graded racing over their next few runs is a form indicator which every backer should bear in mind.

SYSTEM FIVE

How to land really big forecast dividends for only three tickets per race

What would happen if you backed every dog in every race at a meeting? Would you win or lose? 'Lose, of course,' is no doubt your reply, and most of the time you would be right. But take a look at this set of results from a recent evening's sport at Walthamstow:

1 point on every dog in every race

			Points outlay	Points return
1st race Winner	5–1		6	6
2nd race Winner	3–1		6	4
3rd race Winner	7–2		6	4½
4th race Winner	7–1		6	8
5th race Winner	7–1		6	8
6th race Winner	14–1		6	15
7th race Winner	6–1		6	7
8th race Winner	3–1		6	4
9th race Winner	10–1		6	11
10th race Winner	4–1		6	5
11th race Winner	9–2		6	5½
12th race Winner	11–4		6	3¾
			72	81¾

Profit: 9¾ points

45

Now I am not suggesting that the backer should follow such a strategy at an actual meeting, although freak results like the above do crop up rather more often than perhaps you might think. Most of the time, however, blanket coverage of this kind would be financial suicide, but there is a serious point. The overall profit was made possible by the unusually large number of good-priced winners, including a couple of rank outsiders. Does this mean, therefore, that the punter in search of a profit from greyhound racing should ignore the fancied dogs and back only longshots?

To find out I conducted a survey of a thousand races at one of the sport's leading venues. An arbitrary date was fixed for the start of the test, and the result of each race added to the figures as it occurred until the quota of one thousand races was reached. All the races in the sample were included whatever the result with two exceptions. First, the tiny number of dead-heats were omitted because they would have tended to confuse things in an exercise designed to give a clear, uncomplicated picture of the pattern of results. Second, open races were ignored, since most tracks, especially in the provinces, feature mainly graded races, and open racing is really a separate branch of the sport. What finally emerged is a unique profile of the greyhound scene from a betting angle.

1000 GRADED RACES. 1 *point on every dog in every race*

	Number of winners	Average Tote odds	Points outlay	Points return	Points loss
FAV.	319	13–8	1000	832	−168
2ND FAV.	224	11–4	1000	836	−164
3RD FAV.	164	4–1	1000	826	−174

4TH FAV.	148	5–1	1000	877	−123
5TH FAV.	94	13–2	1000	725	−275
OUTSIDER	51	9–1	1000	514	−486
	1000		6000	4610	−1390

Note that for the sake of clarity the average odds shown in the table are to the decimal place which most nearly converts to standard betting prices. This accounts for the slight discrepancy in each case between the number of winners and the rate of odds on the one hand, and the actual points return on the other.

Also Tote odds were used rather than the starting prices of the bookmakers. Bookmakers have a tendency to mark up two or three dogs, and especially those in the middle range of the betting, at exactly the same price. This makes it impossible to establish a precise order of favouritism in a narrow market. With the Tote, however, it is always possible to differentiate between each market position by examining just before the off the number of units staked in the pool and the resultant prices as they appear on the Tote betting board or TV screens, and this was how the survey was painstakingly compiled. Quite apart from this, the commission taken by the Totalisator from its pools frequently compares very well with the big advantage in their own favour that the bookmakers incorporate into their prices on a great many races. It is never a bad idea, therefore, to think exclusively in terms of Tote betting. This applies particularly where the less fancied dogs are concerned.

The results of the survey make it possible to draw a number of highly significant betting conclusions:

i) Following any position in the market will produce a loss in the long term.

ii) First, second and third favourites all showed roughly the same amount of loss in the period under review, something in the order of 16–17%, although the two market leaders accounted for 543 winners between them, giving a very high strike rate of 54%.

iii) The very worst dog to back in a six-dog race is the complete outsider.

iv) The best dog to back from the entire range of market positions is the one quoted fourth in the betting. It showed only a marginal loss on the one thousand-race sequence.

If the punter is going to concentrate on dogs at the longer prices in the betting, therefore, it is the fourth-quoted animal which clearly holds out the best prospect of success. On the other hand it could well prove extremely difficult in practice to convert the small loss recorded in the survey into a worthwhile profit. Selective form criteria might help, but with dogs of this type there would be a very real danger of cutting out too many good winners when the punter tries to pick and choose between them.

However there is an old ploy which might help. This is to take the selection for a win 'with the field' to be second in forecasts. So if the backer has £5 to invest on a race, he can opt to have five £1 forecasts, one of which is bound to succeed if the win selection comes in first. In this way he often, but not always, secures a better return for his money than from a straight £5 win bet on his main fancy. Much depends on the type of dog which runs second.

This idea is the basis of the method recommended here, but it is applied selectively, leaving the favourite and the rank outsider out of the bet. Most backers include the favourite in their forecast wagers and when it finishes in the first two, dividends are poor. The complete outsider is omitted for obvious reasons. As the survey shows, it is always very bad business in any six-dog race, and what applies to its winning potential is also true of its chances of coming second.

So the system bet is as follows. Very shortly before the start of each race examine the Tote betting indicator to identify the exact order of favouritism, and then purchase three tickets according to this pattern:

Three 1-point forecasts: 4th Fav./2nd Fav.
4th Fav./3rd Fav.
4th Fav./5th Fav.

Forecast betting at most tracks is based on a 20p or 25p unit, and the system need not be expensive with never more than a few pounds at risk during the whole course of a meeting.

However, apart from the occasional exceptional meeting, most of the time the bet will not find a lot of winning forecasts from the typical twelve-race graded card. According to the survey, the fourth-quoted dog wins about 15% of all races, which means a minimum expectation of one to two winners from the entire programme. Therefore the system operator does not push his luck. As soon as he lands a winning forecast, he ceases betting for the rest of the card. The dividend is nearly certain to be a handsome one and should be good enough to show a sound profit even when the successful bet does not come up until late in the proceedings.

If the fourth-quoted dog fails to turn up at any point, or if it wins with the favourite or complete outsider second on those occasions it is first past the post, there will be a total loss. This will happen now and again and when it does, it is a failure that must be accepted as one of those things in a sport where no method can be devised which guarantees the backer will win every time. In this circumstance the system operator should double his stakes *for the next meeting only* in an attempt to recoup losses and continue on the road to a long term profit.

The above formula is so cheap to work that it is ideal for use alongside other methods being operated at the same meeting. When it wins it could well make up for losses from other bets on a bad afternoon or night, whilst supplementing gains nicely at those times when everything else the punter does comes off. As a back-up bet or a method with a high winning potential in its own right, it is a valuable additional weapon for anyone in the battle to show a regular profit.

SYSTEM SIX

A trap number system for regular winning forecasts

Trap number systems are very popular amongst all sorts of greyhound fans. Many who only visit the track occasionally for an afternoon or evening out, knowing little of current form, like to 'play the numbers'. On the other hand some number enthusiasts go to enormous trouble and keep detailed records of trap success and failure over a series of previous meetings, in the hope of discovering from sequences of numbers clues about likely future trends. Trap number systems are also worked down the card at a single meeting in the belief that early results hold the key to what will happen later on in the programme.

It must be said straightaway that systems based on winning and losing runs of numbers are mathematically unsound. In say, a six-dog race, leaving aside considerations of form and any other factors which may affect performance, in purely mathematical terms it is exactly 5–1 against, no more and no less, that any trap will win. This is true regardless of what has gone before. So if at a particular meeting, trap 2 has been successful six times in a row, in the next race it has exactly the same mathematical chance of winning as any of the other five traps – the so-called 'law of averages' operating against its chance simply does not apply. This is also the case with losing sequences. When say, trap 5 fails to win any of the first eleven races on the card, that in itself is no reason why it should win the twelfth.

Trap betting is also founded on other preconceptions. Some who bet on forecasts try to predict the 1–2 result by combining patterns of odd- and even-numbered traps. This idea has no logical basis in mathematics and is only coincidentally borne out by results in the short term. Over an extended period there is absolutely nothing in the odd/even theory.

Many trap bettors swear by the idea of backing dogs running from adjacent traps. If they can identify the probable winner, they argue, the dogs drawn on either side are likely to be pulled along by the fastest dog, and should be included in forecasts. Now anyone who has watched even a few greyhound races will realise that this notion, though a popular one, has very little in it. So much can happen in an actual contest, especially at the bends, that the opening positions of the runners are quickly blurred beyond all recognition. If the dogs raced like human athletes in a 100 metres dash along clearly separated lanes, there might be something in the idea, but four bends on an oval track is what greyhound racing is all about and of course accounts for much of the difficulty in forecasting results accurately. Masses of returns from up and down the country demonstrate quite clearly that the arguments in favour of forecast betting on dogs in adjoining boxes are not supported by the statistical evidence.

However there is such a thing as trap bias. In any race there is always a small, but discernible, in-built advantage to some boxes over others at certain tracks. Take for example this set of statistics which cover a long period of racing in the year that I write at one of the afternoon BAGS meetings, Hackney:

	1	2	3	4	5	6
Firsts	210	144	164	165	146	210
Seconds	209	179	165	158	155	173

And another example, this time from Bristol:

	1	2	3	4	5	6
Firsts	153	121	130	113	112	93
Seconds	150	124	118	101	112	116

Clearly the bias in favour of traps 1 and 6 at Hackney, and the advantage to the inside box at Bristol, is just too pronounced to be mere coincidence, and is no doubt explained by the conformation of the courses. Although both cases are exceptional, the Hackney figures in particular do confirm a general tendency not confined to just one track, but which applies to all greyhound sport, namely that the dogs in the inside and outside boxes start with a slight edge over their rivals. Unlike the rest of the field, both the 1 dog and the 6 dog have just one animal at their side, and provided they can hold their place reasonably well at the first bend, they are at risk of being bumped by only a single runner not two. The dog in the inside box has the rails and the shortest distance to travel of all the competitors. The trap 6 dog has the farthest to go, but if it runs wide, has the best chance of avoiding the scrimmaging which nearly always occurs as the dogs battle to clear the all-important first corner. The poor performance of the outside runner at Bristol is something of a mystery, and may simply be due to the lack of quality of the wide runners currently competing there.

Be that as it may, the bias in favour of wide runners at all tracks becomes even more pronounced in periods of wet weather. When it rains heavily the softened ground gets churned up near the rails where most of the action takes place. So as a meeting progresses, the runners from the outside boxes avoid the worst of the going, and this is often reflected in the pattern of results.

Having noted the phenomenon of trap bias, however, it would be wrong to go on from there and attempt to formulate a whole theory of betting from it. In the long run every trap supplies its share of winners, and in all races a good dog given reasonable luck in running can overcome any slight disadvantage arising from its starting position.

The real plus in favour of betting on trap numbers lies in their impartiality in regard to form, times and the betting market. So by following a trap number, or some combination of them, the backer is as much likely to find long-priced winners as successful short-priced favourites. This set of results from a recent London meeting illustrates the point. There is nothing freakish about them and similar patterns can be found almost any day.

Results for trap 5

1st race	lost	7th	race	lost
2nd race	won 5–4	8th	race	lost
3rd race	lost	9th	race	won 8–1
4th race	won 11–2	10th	race	lost
5th race	won 6–1	11th	race	won 3–1
6th race	lost	12th	race	lost

Five winners here for anyone who had decided, for whatever reason, to follow trap 5 throughout the programme. The punter who makes his selections on form on the other hand, would have been very unlikely to have backed winners at 11–2, 6–1 and 8–1. In fact most form students would have been well content to have found five winners at much lesser prices.

But this does not mean that trap number betting should necessarily be divorced from orthodox selection methods. If a system can be devised which combines the advantages of impartial sequences of trap numbers with some viable form factor, then the backer may well get the best of both worlds.

The method recommended here is based in the first instance on the selections of press experts. These men regularly attend their local tracks and know the dogs in the kennels inside out. Their opinion about the outcome of any race is worthy of the highest respect. A lengthy survey of their efforts at all kinds of meetings in different parts of the country revealed that if two experts' choices for the same card are taken in combination, then over an extended period they find the winner of about 70% of all races from their main and danger tips. Given the fact that the vast majority of newspaper correspondents maintain roughly the same high standard, clearly such an excellent strike rate is just too good to be passed over lightly.

What has this got to do with trap numbers? Well, if you know how, it is in fact not difficult to use press selections to identify at any meeting which of the traps from 1 to 6, or which of the boxes at tracks that feature five-dog races, carry the most fancied animals taking the card as a whole.

Here is an imaginary set of selections from two experts at a twelve-race meeting:

Expert A

	Selection	Trap	Danger	Trap
1st race	Green Plover	6	Flashing Up	2
2nd race	Lucky Dog	1	Honda Racer	5
3rd race	Dawn Skiddy	3	Faraway Jet	2
4th race	Proud Pet	2	Big Billy	1
5th race	Date My Darling	3	Rose Stuart	6
6th race	Time And Again	4	Four Wheel	2
7th race	Chaseaway	1	Dumbo Crambo	5
8th race	Grande Dame	4	John's Pride	5
9th race	Tory Tip	6	Tiger Moth	3
10th race	Welcome Home	4	Valley Jet	1
11th race	Showtime	4	Dutch Painter	1
12th race	Star Sailor	5	Brown Lucky	6

Expert B

	Selection	Trap	Danger	Trap
1st race	Flashing Up	2	Going To Town	4
2nd race	Rough Line	2	Milady's Pearl	4
3rd race	Iron Black	6	Go For Broke	1
4th race	Big Billy	1	Proud Pet	2
5th race	Rose Stuart	6	Whitney Champion	4
6th race	Smile Four	5	Salvador	3
7th race	Chaseaway	1	Slim Girl	6
8th race	Grande Dame	4	John's Pride	5
9th race	Desperate Dilly	1	Fun Time	2
10th race	Valley Jet	1	Welcome Home	4
11th race	Come On Jane	3	Dutch Painter	1
12th race	Star Sailor	5	Pride of Corran	1

The idea of the system is to award 1 point to a trap if it is occupied by a dog given as a selection or danger by either expert. If both tipsters choose the same dog as one of their picks, the duplication is ignored at this stage and the trap from which it runs still receives just 1 point.

Thus in the first race in the example Expert A fancies Green Plover and names Flashing Up as his danger. Expert B nominates Flashing Up as his first selection with Going To Town next best. Green Plover is in trap 6, Flashing Up is in trap 2 and Going To Town occupies 4. So in the opening event traps 2, 4 and 6 are favoured. The points would be allocated like this:

Trap 1	Trap 2	Trap 3	Trap 4	Trap 5	Trap 6
	1		1		1

In the next race one expert gives Lucky Dog (trap 1) to win with Honda Racer (trap 5) as his danger. The other goes for Rough Line (trap 2) and Milady's Pearl (trap 4). The allocation in the second race would be:

Trap 1	Trap 2	Trap 3	Trap 4	Trap 5	Trap 6
1	1		1	1	

If this principle of converting selections and dangers to the traps they run from is carried on down the card, then it becomes possible to arrive at an order of likely success for the traps over the meeting in its entirety.

The conversion for all twelve races would look like this:

	Trap 1	Trap 2	Trap 3	Trap 4	Trap 5	Trap 6
Race 1		1		1		1
Race 2	1	1		1	1	
Race 3	1	1	1			1
Race 4	1	1				
Race 5			1	1		1
Race 6		1	1	1	1	
Race 7	1				1	1
Race 8				1	1	
Race 9	1	1	1			1
Race 10	1			1		
Race 11	1		1	1		
Race 12	1				1	1
	8	6	5	7	5	6

According to the chart, therefore, trap 1 has the best chance of turning up the greatest number of firsts and seconds at the meeting. It has eight nominations as selection or danger from the two experts. Trap 4 with seven tips comes next, and 2 and 6 are joint third with six each.

The system operates on the three most favoured traps at six-dog tracks, and on the two top boxes where the programme is entirely or largely made up of contests for just five dogs. Sometimes the formula will give you a clear order of merit straightaway. At other times it will be necessary to break a tie between the highest totals in order to arrive at the system traps. With five dogs you will always need to separate the best two traps from the rest. When there are six dogs in a race, there has to be a clear distinction between the top two traps, the third best and the remainder of the boxes. The recommended procedure is as follows: for traps which have an equal number of votes, go back over the tips, and take the trap which has the highest number of first choices, as opposed to dangers, from the two experts; if there is still a tie, the trap that contains the most dogs mentioned by both tipsters as a main selection or as a danger is preferred. In the initial count, remember, no distinction was made between selections and dangers, and a dog picked by both tipsters earned only 1 point for the trap it occupied. Now ties are broken by adding up the number of clear main choices in the first instance, and then, if necessary, by taking into account any duplicated tips.

In our example traps 1 and 4 are clearly the best two traps, but with six dogs per race, an outright third choice is required from traps 2 and 6. From trap 2, Expert A gave Proud Pet as a main selection, and Expert B Flashing Up and Rough Line, three first choices for the trap. But trap 6 has four – Green Plover and Tory Tip from Expert A, and Iron Black and Rose Stuart from Expert B. Trap 6, therefore, is preferred, and there is no need to count duplicated tips.

Having established the order of merit for the traps, the system bets in each race are:

Six-dog tracks

Four forecasts:
Top trap to win/next best to be second
Next best to win/top trap to be second
Top trap to win/third best to be second
Next best to win/third best to be second

So in the example the actual bets would be:

Reversed forecast 1–4 (2 units)
Straight forecast 1–6 (1 unit)
Straight forecast 4–6 (1 unit)

Five-dog tracks

Two forecasts:
Top trap to win/next best to be second
Next best to win/top trap to be second

The actual bet is:

Reversed forecast 1–4 (2 units)

On six-dog tracks, therefore, four forecast combinations are backed; where there are five runners per race, the bet is a reversed forecast on just two traps. The reason for the difference is that it is much more difficult to find successful forecasts when six dogs take part in a race. Four bets in each event give good prospects of a dividend without sacrificing profitability. In five-dog races, however, there are only twenty possible combinations of numbers for 1–2 forecasts, with the result that on average dividends are lower. It would not be economic to lay out four units every time. So here the bet is two numbers only to finish first or second in either order.

The system may give its followers many winning forecasts over an extended period of betting, but the backer must be wary of being greedy. The favoured traps carry his money down the card. However they will not turn up in every race, very far from it. In fact the system operates on what might be called the principle of minimum expectation. The six-dog method requires the operator to bet from race to race only until he has drawn one dividend from his reversed forecast. Thereafter it is abandoned for the remainder of the meeting. From his two straight forecasts also, he looks for just one win. Again, as soon as he draws a dividend, he stops betting on either of them during the rest of the programme.

Likewise with the bet in five-dog races, when the system is to stop at a win after one successful forecast.

This limited approach will not result in fantastic profits, but provided the dividends that accrue are reasonable ones, there is a good chance of an overall gain at a meeting, even when the system numbers do not turn up until well down the card. If you get lucky early on, it is temping to go on betting in every race, but this is a temptation that must be resisted. Should further successes follow, and it is far from certain that they will, stakes from losing races may well eat into any subsequent gain. Most of the time going beyond the minimum expectation is not worth the risk. Far better to pocket your winnings and wait for another meeting. There are plenty of other methods in this book which can be used in conjunction with the plan for those occasions when early success leaves you with no interest in the remainder of the programme.

Although restricted in its aims, the formula is a carefully planned way of betting for profit in the difficult field of forecasts. It is not certain to win at every meeting, for greyhound racing is by definition a gamble, but by backing those traps which according to the independent opinion of two experts carry the most dogs with the best potential, the backer gives himself a really sound chance of regular wins. The plan will produce good-priced winners and placers as well as animals at short odds, for the system numbers are followed through the card regardless of the original tips for individual races, form or the betting market. From time to time, therefore, a mammoth dividend can result from two unfancied runners not selected for their race by the two experts and disregarded by other punters.

Here what an old greyhound 'pro' once called the 'C' factor emerges as the backer's biggest ally. 'C' stands for consistency, and it is a sad fact of life that many greyhound fans are not consistent in their betting tactics. They tend to get discouraged easily and react by jumping around from one expedient to another. What nearly always happens is that they fall between two stools, missing the winners that would have stemmed from a consistent strategy. By contrast the above method is very much governed by the 'C' factor. By concentrating on favoured traps and faithfully sticking to them, it offers the punter the optimum chance of eventually striking a win and takes a lot of the uncertainty out of betting. In the hands of a disciplined operator, it may well prove a real money-spinner.

SYSTEM SEVEN

How to back favourites with maximum prospects of steady gains

We have already seen that following favourites indiscriminately is not the way to make greyhound racing pay. On the other hand the betting market is a valuable guide to what could well happen in a race, and there is no doubt that careful observation of market trends can provide a lot of significant clues. Outlined in this chapter is a way of backing favourites by which the backer can make an acceptable, if unspectacular profit at many, many meetings from a limited number of bets. It works consistently well because it is based on patterns of results which according to statistics recur over and over again. It is also highly selective in its approach and has nothing to do with blindly plunging on favourites just because they are favourites, a tactic that usually leads to disaster.

It is a fact that at every greyhound track, week in, week out, year after year, favourites in graded as well as open races are placed first or second in one of every two six-dog races, and even more often in five-dog contests. Of course the 50% strike rate may fluctuate on a short series of races at an individual meeting, but viewing the mass of statistics as a whole, this remarkable average is always maintained. Moreover place dividends on favourites are frequently very generous. The reason is that most of the money in the Tote pool goes on the favourite to win – few punters think it worthwhile backing an animal at a short price for a place. As a result place dividends for favourites are often only slightly less than the returns for an outright win. Amazing as it may seem, on occasion the place dividend from a successful favourite can be higher than the dividend for a win. Such are the quirks of betting on the Tote!

As a general policy, therefore, it makes sense to back market leaders for a place only and to forego the win bet altogether. No one will ever get rich by this means, but small regular gains should never be scoffed at and may well tide the punter over an otherwise poor meeting when the rest of his wagers work out badly.

It is a feature of greyhound racing how in any series of risks at the lower end of the odds range, winners and losers tend to alternate. Prolonged series of winning or losing hazards are rare. This is true in the obvious cases of odds on favourites and newspaper naps, and it is exactly the same when market leaders are backed for a place only. It is not surprising when you think about it. Consider the even chances at roulette. Except for freak patterns, a reasonable number of spins of the wheel will see neither long runs of consecutive wins or losses for black or red. Rather the reds and the blacks will be mixed up in fairly equal proportions, with no colour predominating in an unbroken winning sequence of any great length. This is the very opposite of what happens in the case of trap numbers where a one in six chance in every race often produces extended blank periods for one number or another.

When place betting on greyhound favourites, therefore, it is logical to try to anticipate the pattern of alternating winners and losers which dominates series of chances at short odds. By contrast, sequences of the other kind are highly improbable, as in this example of a twelve-race card where placed favourites maintain exactly the one success in two ratio:

Race 1	UNPLACED
Race 2	UNPLACED
Race 3	UNPLACED
Race 4	UNPLACED
Race 5	UNPLACED
Race 6	UNPLACED
Race 7	PLACED
Race 8	PLACED
Race 9	PLACED
Race 10	PLACED
Race 11	PLACED
Race 12	PLACED

Or:

Race 1	UNPLACED
Race 2	UNPLACED
Race 3	UNPLACED
Race 4	PLACED
Race 5	PLACED
Race 6	PLACED
Race 7	UNPLACED
Race 8	UNPLACED
Race 9	UNPLACED
Race 10	PLACED
Race 11	PLACED
Race 12	PLACED

Much more likely is this sort of thing:

Race 1	UNPLACED
Race 2	PLACED

Race 3	UNPLACED
Race 4	PLACED
Race 5	PLACED
Race 6	UNPLACED
Race 7	PLACED
Race 8	UNPLACED
Race 9	UNPLACED
Race 10	PLACED
Race 11	UNPLACED
Race 12	PLACED

Given the prevalence of patterns of the above kind, the recommended method of staking for place bets on favourites is as follows:

Betting through the card, only back a favourite for a place if the favourite in the previous race was unplaced. Treat each meeting separately, i.e. do not carry sequences over from one meeting to the next.

Since bookmakers will not accept place only bets, wagers are made with the Tote, and the favourite is defined as the runner at the shortest odds on the Tote's betting indicator immediately before the start of a race.

It is not likely that one of the freak patterns set out above will occur very often, but let us examine how the staking method fares on such unfavourable sequences. First:

UNPLACED, UNPLACED, UNPLACED,
UNPLACED, UNPLACED, UNPLACED, PLACED,
PLACED, PLACED, PLACED, PLACED, PLACED

This would yield five losing races (second to sixth in the sequence) for the recommended staking procedure, and only one success (seventh race) for a sizeable loss on the series of wagers.

Now the second improbable turn-up:

UNPLACED, UNPLACED, UNPLACED, PLACED,
PLACED, PLACED, UNPLACED, UNPLACED,
UNPLACED, PLACED, PLACED, PLACED

Here the bet would lose on races two, three, eight and nine, and win on races four and ten. So in spite of the freak pattern, there are four failures and two successes, not a bad result in the circumstances.

However things improve dramatically on the typical sort of sequence set out above. That was:

UNPLACED, PLACED, UNPLACED, PLACED,
PLACED, UNPLACED, PLACED, UNPLACED,
UNPLACED, PLACED, UNPLACED, PLACED

This is much better, for the staking would produce wins in races two, four, seven, ten and twelve, with only one loser in race nine, a ratio of five to one in its favour.

It would be wrong to expect results like this on every card, but if you experiment with the returns from a few past meetings, you will see that most of the time the right kinds of patterns do occur. Of course when the percentage of placed favourites falls below the statistical expectation of 50%, the picture is much less attractive, but even then a complete loss is not likely. Here is an example where only four favourites are placed:

UNPLACED, UNPLACED, UNPLACED, PLACED,
PLACED, UNPLACED, UNPLACED, PLACED,
UNPLACED, PLACED, UNPLACED, UNPLACED

In this case the plan loses at races two, three, seven and twelve, but wins at races four, eight and ten – only four placed favourites, but still three winning bets against four losing ones.

Finally to give an idea of the profit potential of the scheme, I show the results from an actual meeting I attended recently. It is absolutely typical, and has not been singled out simply because it puts the system in a favourable light.

FAVOURITE. *£2 for a place*

			Stake	Dividend	Profit	Loss
Race 1		Unplaced				
Race 2	BET HERE	Won	£2	£6.12	£4.12	
Race 3		Unplaced				
Race 4	BET HERE	Second	£2	£3.28	£1.28	
Race 5		Unplaced				
Race 6	BET HERE	Unplaced	£2			£2
Race 7	BET HERE	Unplaced	£2			£2
Race 8	BET HERE	Unplaced	£2			£2
Race 9	BET HERE	Won	£2	£4.96	£2.96	
Race 10		Unplaced				
Race 11	BET HERE	Won	£2	£6.80	£4.80	
Race 12		Second				
		5 placed			£13.16	£6
		7 unplaced				

Profit overall: £7.16

68

The arguments in favour of this plan are so striking that some adventurous readers might get carried away and decide to stake very large sums on the idea. Remember, however, that untypical patterns do turn up from time to time, and a series of hefty wagers would lead to a huge loss on just one bad sequence. Moderate stakes on the other hand may produce steady gains which in the long term could add up to a reasonable credit balance.

SYSTEM EIGHT

The very best bets from your newspaper

The work of the specialist greyhound correspondents whose selections appear in newspapers for the price of a few pence is always worthy of close inspection by any punter. These men are seasoned experts who follow the racing at their local tracks very closely, and their knowledge of the form of individual dogs is unlikely to be equalled by even the most enthusiastic of racegoers, for their press credentials make them very much insiders of the sport.

But just how good are they at picking winners? We have already seen how blanket coverage of a meeting by a couple of these experts produces a very high average of winners. Is it possible to go further and perhaps identify trends which could provide very specific pointers in the search for consistent profits from greyhound racing? To find out I conducted a survey based on tips which are regularly featured in one national newspaper for the afternoon BAGS meetings. Although confined to a single tipster, this may be taken as a fair test, for the level of expertise between one press expert and another probably varies very little. One hundred BAGS meetings were examined in detail, a big enough sample to make the outcome of the survey reasonably definitive.

What emerged demonstrates quite clearly that if the punter concentrates on the selections of a reliable newspaper man, he will have a ready source of winners. In fact an average of just over six winners per twelve-race meeting was indicated by the main and danger selections taken together, the first choice achieving an overall success rate of 27% and the danger only just behind with 24%. Obviously therefore, the backer who is intent on following the tips of a chosen newspaper correspondent should not rely exclusively on his principal selections. Second choices in any race are likely to do almost as well, and also start at better odds much of the time.

This opens up several possible approaches for systematic betting. The views of a number of experts could be examined, taking into account both their main and danger fancies, and a clear choice arrived at according to the consensus of opinion. The trouble with the consensus idea is that it will nearly always indicate the favourite in any race. Moreover there is no real guarantee that the majority vote will be more successful over an extended period than following just one tipster through thick and thin. There might be a marginally higher percentage of winners, but consistently shorter starting prices would almost certainly eat into any increased profit potential.

Another approach would be to back both the main and danger selections of a single tipster in the same race and attempt to win by adjusting stakes according to price. This is technically difficult, and in greyhound racing where the fact that there are only a few runners means the odds are always on the short side, it is doubtful whether a consistent profit could be conjured from regularly backing one third of a six-dog field.

This definitely applies to betting down the card from race to race, but take a look at this layout:

Race 1   Selection/Danger
Race 2   Selection/Danger
Race 3   Selection/Danger

Cover for 8 trebles

Suppose the winners of all three races are found by one or other of the two tips, each at the moderate odds of say, only 3–1. This would give a winning treble of 63–1 and a profit on outlay of no less than 56 points. Of course the bet loses completely unless the three winners are included, but multiple wagers of this sort can reap handsome dividends, given a good source of successful selections. Newspaper selections are just such a source, and there is absolutely no reason why they should not be linked effectively to the above format, although clearly from a twelve-race programme it is necessary to be selective.

A thorough study of press selections in general suggests that newspaper tipsters are consistently more successful with certain types of selection and in certain sorts of races. They do best in terms of percentage of winners in open races, but prices tend to be on the very short side and in any case most greyhound cards consist of graded events. Also they do very well with their naps, even on graded cards. As for the kind of events where they excel, it is possible to detect a higher rate of success at the lowest level of graded racing. It seems the worse the class of the race, the better they do. At practically every track the first two races on the card are for dogs in the lowest grades, and it is on these that the present method concentrates. This is contrary to the preferences of most greyhound followers. These events tend to be generally despised and many racegoers do not even bother to arrive at the stadium in time for them. Yet in a low-grade event early in the programme it is often possible to pick out at least one reasonably consistent dog with enough ability to beat a very poor collection of rivals.

The system bet, therefore, is as follows:

8 points	Correspondent's nap selection for the meeting
1st race:	Selection/Danger
2nd race:	Selection/Danger
	Nap/Danger to Nap

Cover for 8 1-point trebles

Total stake: 16 points

A point can be whatever the backer likes – 10p, 25p, 50p or some other basic unit. If the nap is down to run in one of the two opening races on the card, the normal 8 points is staked on it to win and the correspondent's next best for the meeting and the danger to it are substituted as the third leg of the treble.

The ultimate aim of the bet is always to land a winning treble, but since newspaper naps often show a level stakes profit in their own right, the chosen tipster's best selection is covered with a stake equal to the outlay on the trebles as a form of insurance. Also the danger to the nap selection frequently wins when the nap itself is beaten, and this is included as part of the trebles wager.

Below are ten sample results taken from the survey. They show good results for the system and bad ones, and are included to give readers some idea of what to expect from the plan.

1st race:	Selection lost/Danger lost
2nd race:	Selection won 5–1/Danger lost
	Nap won 5–2/Danger to Nap lost
	Profit: 12 points

1st race:	Selection won 5–2/Danger lost
2nd race:	Selection won 7–4/Danger lost
	Nap lost/Danger to Nap won 5–1
	Profit: 41¾ points

1st race:	Selection lost/Danger lost
2nd race:	Selection lost/Danger won 7–2
	Nap lost/Danger to Nap won 6–4
	Loss: 16 points

1st race:	Selection lost/Danger lost
2nd race:	Selection lost/Danger lost
	Nap lost/Danger to Nap won 3–1
	Loss: 16 points

1st race:	Selection won 7–4/Danger lost
2nd race:	Selection won 5–2/Danger lost
	Nap lost/Danger to Nap won Evens
	Profit: 3¼ points

1st race:	Selection lost/Danger lost
2nd race:	Selection lost/Danger won 5–2
	Nap lost/Danger to Nap lost
	Loss: 16 points

| 1st race: | Selection lost/Danger lost |
| 2nd race: | Selection lost/Danger won 7–2 |

Nap won 6–4/Danger to Nap lost
Profit: 4 points

1st race:	Selection lost/Danger lost
2nd race:	Selection lost/Danger lost
	Nap won 3–1/Danger to Nap lost
	Profit: 16 points

1st race:	Selection won 11–4/Danger lost
2nd race:	Selection won 9–4/Danger lost
	Nap won 6–4/Danger to Nap lost
	Profit: 34½ points

1st race:	Selection won 6–4/Danger lost
2nd race:	Selection won 3–1/Danger lost
	Nap lost/Danger to Nap lost
	Loss: 16 points

From the above it is clear that a lot depends on turning up a winning treble from time to time, and given the wastage in stakes of 8 points whenever the treble fails to win, some readers might prefer to use their skill as judges of form to pick out just one dog for each race. Three selections could then be backed in singles, doubles and a treble. Such a wager may produce larger profits in the long run, although the advantage of backing two dogs per race would be sacrificed and a high degree of forecasting skill would obviously be required. Whatever the preference of individual readers, however, the ideas set out in this chapter could well produce some profitable betting by exploiting the undoubted expertise of newspaper correspondents who are professionals paid to find winners.

SYSTEM NINE

Big wins for small stakes

Every backer dreams of winning a very large sum for a very small outlay. The superoptimist regularly tries to turn the dream into reality, whilst even many naturally cautious punters are not really immune and go for a big 'touch' from time to time. Sadly few of these bets succeed, for the simple reason that the odds against them are so long. In greyhound racing there are traditionally two ways of attempting the elusive goal: forecast doubles and trebles, and permutation bets of the 'Yankee' type. For a number of reasons the two kinds of wager are not equally good from the punter's point of view.

In a forecast double or treble, the backer is required to nominate the first two in correct order in each of two or each of three races. It is no exaggeration to say that these bets are a fool's paradise. Even though there are only six dogs per race, it is in fact far more difficult to name the first and second in a double event than it at first appears, and to perform the same feat in three races calls for forecasting skill bordering on the clairvoyant. A permutation can help provided it is reasonably inexpensive, but even when some arrangement of multiple forecasts is employed, the mathematical chance against landing a forecast double or treble is nearly always significantly greater than the return from the 'Computer Straight Forecast', the mechanism of their own invention by which bookmakers calculate winning bets. The backer only gains against the true mathematical odds when three or four dogs win or are placed at long prices, and even then he does not receive full value for the starting price returns by the Computer Straight Forecast manipulation.

At many tracks the equivalent wager is the Quinela in which the punter has to name the first two in either order in each of three specified races. This is operated like other Tote pools and is perfectly fair. Dividends that represent genuine value for money are frequently paid for a difficult but by no means impossible forecasting challenge. But the bookmakers' version is definitely a bet to avoid. During a recent visit to a High Street betting shop I counted no less than five prominently displayed printed slips to accommodate various forecast double and forecast treble wagers. If bookmaking firms are so keen to promote these bets, then the obvious and cynical conclusion has to be drawn: they are strictly for the 'mug' punter whose business bookmakers will always go out of their way to attract.

There is another good reason why forecast bets of this type are positively bad for the punter. They are 'all or nothing' bets. They are either win or lose, and there are no consolation prizes. So in a forecast double, the backer can for example correctly pick the 1–2 in the first leg and also name the winner in the second, but if he does not find the placed dog as well, he is a complete loser. Likening the bet to the conventional sort of wager, he has in effect found three 'winners' for which he receives absolutely no credit.

This is not the case when a number of dogs are backed to win in a combination of doubles, trebles and accumulators. Even if some selections lose, depending on the number of winners nominated and their starting prices, the backer will recover some or all of his outlay and may show a profit.

Hence the popularity of the ubiquitous Yankee bet which covers four selections in six doubles, four trebles and an accumulator. It has been estimated that close on a million Yankee bets on dogs and horses are handed over betting shop counters in Britain every single week.

Yet despite the fact that it is staple fare for so many punters, the basic four-selection Yankee has a definite drawback. Although it is potentially a good winner when all the selections succeed, it does far less well when the strike rate falls to 50%, a reasonable expectation for most punters most of the time. So while four winners is all profit and three at only 7–4 on will recover stakes, with better odds producing a gain, if the punter finds just two winners at anything less than 95–40 or 2 ⅜–1 each (one at 9–4 and one at 5–2), the bet shows a loss. When it is remembered that three losers and a winner even at a very big price is a total loser, there is a strong case for saying that the backer would be well advised to eliminate the doubles part of the wager altogether. In fact he will do far better in the long run if he bets in singles alongside the trebles and four-timer of the traditional bet. The 11-point outlay of the conventional Yankee divided up as follows is a far better balanced wager:

> Four selections: Four 1½-point singles
> Four 1-point trebles
> One 1-point accumulator
>
> Outlay: 11 points

If the basic weakness of the four-selection bet is the doubles element, it follows that the same is true of all

Number of selections	Outlay in points	Name	Doubles	Trebles	4-folds	5-f.	6-f.	7-f.	8-f.	9-f.	10-f.	11-f.	12-f.
4	11	YANKEE	6	4	1	–	–	–	–	–	–	–	–
5	26	CANADIAN	10	10	5	1	–	–	–	–	–	–	–
6	57	HEINZ	15	20	15	6	1	–	–	–	–	–	–
7	120	MULTI	21	35	35	21	7	1	–	–	–	–	–
8	247	GOLIATH	28	56	70	56	28	8	1	–	–	–	–
9	502	ATLAS	36	84	126	126	84	36	9	1	–	–	–
10	1013	PLUTO	45	120	210	252	210	120	45	10	1	–	–
11	2036	LEVIATHAN	55	165	330	462	462	330	165	55	11	1	–
12	4083	TITAN	66	220	495	792	924	792	495	220	66	12	1

the bets which extend coverage beyond four selections. In the table below is the entire range of full cover wagers of the Yankee type. The intelligent reader will have no difficulty in making the modifications necessary to transfer stakes from doubles to singles along the lines suggested.

For the sake of completeness all bets of this type are included, although the 'Leviathan' punter who indulges in 'Titanic' bets involving double-figure accumulators is surely guilty of wasting stakes. Realistically six selections on any racing day is a maximum for the sensible punter. Below is a format based on that number which offers excellent prospects of really worthwhile gains even when two or three selections lose.

Six selections: 20 trebles
15 fourfolds
1 sixfold

Outlay: 36 points

No singles or doubles are included, but with six dogs covered there is a good margin of error, and the wager has far more big money potential than the standard Yankee and similar guarantees of acceptable lesser returns. Most of the time the punter will fall short of the six-winner target, but five winners produce ten trebles and five fourfolds, whilst four winners give four trebles and the certainty of a successful accumulator. In a wager involving over three times the stake there is no chance of recovering outlay with three odds on winners as in the conventional four-selection Yankee, but the backer has half as many selections again on his side, and 50% winners at the break-even rate of 95–40 for doubles in the Yankee will yield a slightly better result in this bet.

80

So on a good day this arrangement may bring in a gigantic payout, with plenty of insurance against complete loss when only half the selections win.

Preferences in betting are naturally very much a matter of individual temperament. Not everyone will think it worthwhile to try and nominate six winners, or even four, but for those who are not afraid to chance their arm, this chapter should set them along the right road. It will also steer them away from some of the pitfalls inherent in the usual ways of trying to win really big sums from greyhounds in a single coup.

SYSTEM TEN

Sensible staking methods to help you win

The true test of a good betting system is whether it wins consistently at level stakes. Having said that, a strong case can be made for the use of some sort of staking plan when betting on greyhounds. This is because most of the winners from any well-conceived method of selection will nearly always be at the lower end of the odds range. Even with a good percentage of winners, prices from around 2–1 to 4–1 make a worthwhile profit difficult to generate, either in the short or long term. Below are details of a number of sensible staking methods which have a fair chance of enhancing level stakes gains, and even of converting small losses into a credit balance in the backer's favour. First, however, it is necessary to say a few words about the different types of stakes adjustment available to the punter.

Basically the system operator may increase stakes after losers or after winners, and there are drawbacks to both approaches. Clearly doubling up on a losing run is financial suicide, for sooner or later a long series of unsuccessful bets will bedevil even the soundest system, with the result that the backer's betting funds may well be wiped out. However even staking methods which call for only mild increases on a series of losing selections have definite disadvantages. First, the losing run may be unusually prolonged, or second, the price of the winner which finally breaks the sequence of losers may be too short to recover earlier losses. In either case, or more exactly when both circumstances combine, the gain from the winner may fail to offset accumulated losses from the earlier bets in the series. Regulated increases made on a poor sequence may improve the position when measured against level stakes, but there can be no absolute guarantee of this.

By increasing stakes after winners the punter is on safer ground. He is using money won from the book-maker or the Tote to finance his betting, and provided his winning run continues, he may well end up with a better profit than would have resulted from level stakes on his selections. Even here, however, the situation is not as favourable as it first appears. To be really successful, methods which call for increasing stakes from successful wagers depend to a great extent on unbroken sequences of winners. In practice this favourable type of sequence seldom occurs. What tends to happen is that winners and losers alternate either singly or in small groups. As soon as the punter increases his stakes after a few win-ners, along come two or three losers and all or most of the cash already won from the layers is returned to them. Moreover, even on a good sequence of winners which causes the backer's capital to appreciate rapidly, unless a decision is made to cease betting at some predetermined point, the largest stake will fall on a loser since the winning run must end sometime.

The point about staking plans that most backers fail to understand is that they are completely dependent for their success on the pattern of winners and losers. Since the backer can never know in advance what the exact pattern will be, no staking plan can be devised which will cope with every eventuality to produce a certain gain. In the impossible event of the punter knowing the win/lose pattern before he starts betting, there would be no problem. He would simply back the winners and not bother to put money on the losers.

However this does not mean that staking systems are useless. Provided the method of selection employed can be relied upon to yield a reasonable percentage of winners, and provided volatile increases and decreases in stakes are avoided, staking plans which have limited objectives can often improve on the level stakes position. The plans that follow all fulfil these conditions. Some increase stakes after losers, some are of the type which call for increased outlay from capital accumulated at the expense of the bookmaker or the Tote. The first group is designed for betting at a single meeting treated as a separate entity. The second method is concerned with continuous betting from meeting to meeting.

BETTING AT A SINGLE MEETING

Coup de trois
Many backers prefer to limit themselves to just a few bets per meeting on what they regard as the dogs with the outstanding chances on the card. This staking plan is for a series of three such bets:

> I point on the first selection. If a selection loses at any point, double the stake on the next bet. If a selection wins, stake half the profit from it on the next bet.
>
> Do not bet at odds on. Never extend the sequence beyond three bets.

Here are some examples of this plan in action. A comparison with level stakes is shown in each case.

STAKE	1	1	2
RESULT	2–1	L	L
PROFIT (+) OR LOSS (−)	+2	−1	−2 = −1 point

(Level stakes. Outlay: 4 points ÷ 3 bets = 1 ⅓ points per dog = break even)

STAKE	1	2	2
RESULT	L	2–1	L
PROFIT (+) OR LOSS (−)	−1	+4	−2 = +1 point

(Level stakes. Outlay: 5 points ÷ 3 bets = 1 ⅔ points per dog = break even)

STAKE	1	2	4
RESULT	L	L	2–1
PROFIT (+) OR LOSS (−)	−1	−2	+8 = +5 points

(Level stakes. Outlay: 7 points ÷ 3 bets = 2 ⅓ points per dog = break even)

STAKE	1	1	2
RESULT	2–1	L	4–1
PROFIT (+) OR LOSS (−)	+2	−1	+8 = +9 points

(Level stakes. Outlay: 4 points ÷ 3 bets = 1 ⅓ points per dog = +6 ⅔ points)

STAKE	1	2	2
RESULT	4–1	2–1	2–1
PROFIT (+) OR LOSS (−)	+4	+4	+4 = +12 points

(Level stakes. Outlay: 5 points ÷ 3 bets = 1 ⅔ points per dog = +13⅓ points)

It is emphasised that everything depends on pattern and price, and the above examples are only a selection of the possible combinations of one, two or three winners at the odds of 2–1 and 4–1 I have chosen for the purposes of illustration. However it can be seen that the staking method sometimes improves quite well on the level stakes position, whilst on those occasions when it does worse than levels, there is only a marginal difference in profitability. There is an element of doubling up in the plan, but with a three-bet limit the backer can never lose more than 7 points.

Variable number of bets per meeting

On a short series of bets it is extremely difficult to devise a staking plan that keeps stakes at a reasonable pitch which will regularly improve on the situation at level stakes. However here is a plan for four to twelve bets in sequence which increases stakes gently after losers. Provided the punter finds some winners, there is very little risk in it and it does offer genuine prospects of enchancing profits.

Stake on the progression 1123, reverting to 1 after a winner or four consecutive losers. 1 is 1 point, 2 is 2 points, 3 is 3 points.

Possible patterns of winners and losers and prices are

legion, but here is just one example which illustrates the potential of the formula on a typical series of bets:

```
STAKE    1    1    1    2    3    1    1    1    2    1
RESULT  2–1  L    L    L   2–1 3–1   L    L   4–1   L
PROFIT
(+)
OR LOSS  +2  −1   −1   −2  +6  +3   −1   −1   +8   −1 = +12 points
(−)
```

> (Level stakes. Outlay: 14 points ÷ 10 bets = 1 ⅖ points per dog = +7 points)

To be absolutely fair, this is a sequence where the recommended plan fails when measured against the level stakes test:

```
STAKE    1    1    1    2    3    1    1    1    1    1
RESULT  2–1  L    L    L    L   2–1 3–1   L   4–1   L
PROFIT
(+)
OR LOSS  +2  −1   −1   −2  −3  +2   +3   −1  +4   −1 = +2 points
(−)
```

(Level stakes. Outlay: 13 points ÷ 10 bets = 1 ³/₁₀ points per dog = +6½ points)

However, leaving aside this example which is deliberately framed to present a black picture, it is fair to say that unless the method of selection has a tendency to produce long runs of losers regularly – and no sound system using short- to middle-priced dogs should do so – the recommended procedure will usually enhance any level stakes gain.

Forecast betting

The systems for reversed forecast betting in this book should be operated according to the principle of minimum expectation, whereby the backer ceases betting after a single dividend at a meeting, or in one case after two. However some greyhound fans like a bet in every race. This is not necessarily the best way to make consistent gains, but the sport is not just about winning at all costs. Interest comes into it as well, and for those who share the addiction to reversed forecasts down the card, some mention needs to be made of staking.

In fact no safe or sensible method of adjusting stakes on forecasts has ever been devised. The reason is that dividends are totally unpredictable within the context of a series of bets of any length. Depending on whether short-priced dogs or outsiders get into the frame, some dividends will be very large, others very small, and most somewhere between the two extremes. Given the wide fluctuations that inevitably occur, controlled staking is a virtual impossibility.

There is another reason why the habitual forecast backer should steer clear of staking plans. The mathematical odds against a straight forecast succeeding are 29–1 in a six-dog race and 19–1 in events involving five dogs. Even with a reversed forecast, it is still 14–1 against the backer with six runners and 9–1 when there are five. These odds are prohibitive, and any staking formula which increases stakes after losing races runs the risk of getting into deep trouble very quickly. Similarly a plan that calls for the backer to play up his winnings from race to race is tempting providence to the point where there is always a distinct possibility of sacrificing accumulated capital almost as soon as it has been won. Fractional increases in stakes after winning or losing races may well do little harm, but in the long run will probably produce much the same result as level stakes. Progressions that advance in whole units of the basic stake are courting disaster.

So forecast bettors must recognise that they are in a high risk business where returns fluctuate wildly and unpredictably. If they must bet in lots of races beyond the minimum expectation, they should accept the small payouts alongside the big ones and have nothing to do with plans involving variable integers. On the other hand, there is nothing wrong with carefully re-investing any gain from a single meeting at future ones according to the philosophy outlined in the next section.

CONTINUOUS BETTING FROM MEETING TO MEETING

Trying to win at every meeting is a perfectly legitimate objective but realistically this is not possible, and the backer's best chance of accumulating a worthwhile sum is to bet from meeting to meeting, retaining his winnings and systematically re-investing them for a long term gain. There is no reason why the prudent backer should not do this, employing in isolation the methods set out in the above section. But the problem is that while he carefully regulates stakes on a short sequence of bets at one meeting, he has no automatic means of determining how to wager on subsequent visits to the track. If he is in pocket on his operations as a whole, what proportion of his profit does he risk next time? If he is losing, how does he set about budgeting for recovery of the deficit? Some readers may be content to use their own personal judgement, but it is really far easier to have some method which adjusts stakes from one meeting to the next on a systematic basis. By viewing each individual bet and each individual meeting as part of a whole series, the punter enhances his long term prospects immeasurably.

An old idea is to set aside a sum of money as a bank, and to stake some proportion of it, usually one tenth or one twentieth, on each bet in a series. Thus, with a capital of 100 points and staking one tenth, the initial stake is 10 points. If the best loses, the bank is reduced to 90 points and the next stake will be 9 points, and so on. As winners are backed, the bank may increase and could exceed the original 100 points quite soon. So if the bank reaches 120 points, the next bet would be 12 points. Subsequent winners and losers will cause the amount in the bank to fluctuate, but the backer always places one tenth on any individual bet.

The drawback to this method is that while it will build up a big bank very rapidly on an exceptional run of winners over losers, the typical sequence of results in which quite a few losers as well as winners are backed produces a 'swings and roundabouts' effect. The bank tends to hover around its original amount and never reaches a point where worthwhile increases in stakes are called for. To all intents and purposes most of the time the backer may as well be betting at level stakes.

The following is a more sophisticated and, in the opinion of this writer, a far better idea:

Fix a bank as before, say 100 points. Since one twentieth is a safer rate of increase or decrease than one tenth, divide the bank into twenty units to arrive at the initial stake. Profits from individual bets are added to the bank and losses are deducted. As long as the bank does not exceed the original 100 points, the stake is at the rate of one twentieth of it, that is 5 points *and never drops below 5 points*. If it increases beyond 100 points, the next stake is initially and on all subsequent increases one twentieth, but *once the stake is increased, it is never reduced.*

Thus the opening stake is 5 points, one twentieth of the 100-point bank. If the bank reaches 120 points, the stakes are increased to 6 points. When it reaches 140 points, there is a further increase to a 7-point stake. Should the amount in hand fall back to 120 points, the stake nevertheless remains at 7 points and continues to do so even if the bank is reduced to say, 90 points as the result of a series of losers.

Here is a sample sequence which illustrates the operation of the plan in detail. Stakes are rounded up or down to the nearest 10p, although when betting with a bookmaker at the track it will be necessary to convert this to the nearest pound, since a pound is the basic on course betting unit. Similarly if wagering on the Tote, stakes would be adjusted as near as possible to a multiple of the basic unit stake for Totalisator bets at the particular stadium.

STAKE	RESULT	PROFIT	LOSS	BANK
				£100.00
£5	Won 2–1	£10.00		£110.00
£5.50	Lost		£5.50	£104.50
£5.50	Lost		£5.50	£99.00
£5.50	Lost		£5.50	£93.50
£5.50	Lost		£5.50	£88.00
£5.50	Won 5–1	£27.50		£115.50
£5.80	Lost		£5.80	£109.70
£5.80	Won 4–1	£23.20		£132.90
£6.60	Lost		£6.60	£126.30
£6.60	Lost		£6.60	£119.70
£6.60	Won 2–1	£13.20		£132.90

£6.60	Lost		£6.60	£126.30
£6.60	Won 5–2	£16.50		£142.80
£7.10	Lost		£7.10	£135.70
£7.10	Won 6–4	£10.65		£146.35
£7.30	Lost		£7.30	£139.05
£7.30	Lost		£7.30	£131.75
£7.30	Lost		£7.30	£124.45
£7.30	Lost		£7.30	£117.15
£7.30	Won 5–2	£18.25		£135.40
£7.30	Won 4–1	£29.20		£164.60
£8.20	Won 6–4	£12.30		£176.90
£8.80	Lost		£8.80	£168.10
£8.80	Lost		£8.80	£159.30
£8.80	Won 4–1	£35.20		£194.50
£9.70	Lost		£9.70	£184.80
£9.70	Lost		£9.70	£175.10
£9.70	Won 2–1	£19.40		£194.50
£9.70	Won 3–1	£29.10		£223.60
£11.20	Lost		£11.20	£212.40
£11.20	Lost		£11.20	£201.20
£11.20	Lost		£11.20	£190.00
£11.20	Lost		£11.20	£178.80
£11.20	Lost		£11.20	£167.60
£11.20	Won 3–1	£33.60		£201.20
£11.20	Won 2–1	£22.40		£223.60

So the bank increases from £100 to £223.60 for a profit on the sequence of £123.60. A level £5 on each dog would have yielded a gain of only £85. The staking method has therefore produced a percentage increase over levels of 45%.

This is quite a sound result when it is appreciated that the method is very much a safety first one. Whilst the formula can produce a handsome increase in the size of the bank on only a fairly average sequence of favourable results, its mathematics are such that whatever increase in stake is made, the bank is always in a position to withstand a run of twenty consecutive losers before it is completely broken. However high the stake gets, or in the opposite case of the bank drifting lower and lower on a run of losers mixed with winners whose number and price are not good enough to arrest the downward trend, the backer can never lose more than his original 100-point outlay.

In fact on a really good run the bank and stakes can reach a very high level. Since the object of betting is presumably to make money to spend, some backers may decide to 'check out' after a good gain. For example if the bank reaches 500 points, the system operator might opt to withdraw 200 points and then continue as before. In this case the new bank would be 300 points and the opening stake one twentieth of it, that is 15 points.

Using this method, the backer has no problems in carrying forward his bank from one meeting to the next, whatever the number of his bets on a single card. Even so, there is no substitute for lots of winners and this or any other staking plan by itself is not an automatic road to profit. But provided the punter is able to find a good percentage of winning dogs, the above formula, like the ones explained in the first section of this chapter, offers a reasonable opportunity to increase any gains from his endeavours, without however committing him to levels of staking that run the risk of plunging him headlong into betting ruin.

In concluding this book, it is necessary to say something on the subject of betting on greyhounds in general. Probably the biggest trap for the inexperienced or foolish punter in dog racing are the relatively short odds available about most animals with a chance of winning because of the small number of runners in each race. Staking plans may improve on a level stakes credit balance and produce fair gains over a reasonable period of time, but the only way to make really big profits from singles as opposed to cumulative wagers involving trebles and accumulators is to bet in big stakes. Big stakes can mean big losses, and this no doubt accounts for the evil reputation as a gambling sport which greyhound racing has in some quarters. In this book the reader has been shown sound methods both for selection and staking, but there can be no certainties. The lesson is clear. Bet on the sport in a sensible manner and keep your stakes at a reasonable level. Above all, never bet more than you can comfortably afford to lose. That is the way to get maximum enjoyment from your pastime.